Trio

SIMPLE • BEAUTIFUL • FUN

DECORATING WITH GLASS VASES

Trio

SIMPLE • BEAUTIFUL • FUN

DECORATING WITH GLASS VASES
by Stasia Nawrocki

All you need is . . .

. . . a few cylinder vases with some inserts.

All you do is . . .

. . . use objects around your home and . . . play!
For **INSPIRATION** . . . read on . . . .

Editor: Rita Feutl

Designer: Fiona Santos

Photography: Izabela Wozniak, Marilynn McAra,
Rudolf Zwamborn and Mike Lepatski

Creative Styling Assistant: Tracey Miklejohn

Distributed in Canada by Samaco Trading Ltd.
1-800-263-3093

Printed in Canada by Speedfast Color Press Inc.

Library and Archives Canada Cataloguing in Publication

Nawrocki, Stasia, 1944-
Trio : simple, beautiful, fun decorating with glass vases / Stasia
Nawrocki.

ISBN 0-9781167-0-4

1. Glassware in interior decoration. 2. Vases. I. Title.

NK2115.5.A25N38 2006   747'.9
C2006-903116-9

Published by:
Nawrocki Holdings Ltd.
1510 111 St. N.W.
Edmonton, Alberta
Canada T6J 6T6

For my grandson, Adam, and all brave children
battling a serious illness

Contents

Occasions to Celebrate
Throughout the Seasons

Introduction

There are many elaborate, complicated books about decorating. This is not one of them! *Trio: Simple, Beautiful, Fun—Decorating With Glass Vases* offers easy, eye-catching design ideas that will make you smile and won't take forever to put together.

The material list for each project assumes you have everyday household tools such as scissors and glue guns, and calls for inexpensive decorating equipment and supplies. Indeed, most of the materials used in *Trio: Simple, Beautiful, Fun* can be found in gift shops, craft stores and party supply outlets.

I hope to inspire you, so if you can't find exactly the same bowl or bauble pictured here, don't worry! Create, rather than follow, and use what you have on hand. Substitute your own treasures for the chicks, Santas and other figurines you see on these pages and let each project be your own.

But don't let creativity get in the way of safety. Remember to place candles on stable, secure bases and make sure that flammable materials are kept away from the wick.

Trio: Simple, Beautiful, Fun invites you to experience the delight that inspiration brings. *Enjoy!*

Spring

suddenly spring

Tired of winter? A trip to a local greenhouse will reward you with pots of spring flowers, even though snow still covers the ground. Pick up whatever tickles your fancy – it could be five pots of mini-daffodils, or a variety of spring bulbs. You can create this look instantly or watch the miracle of new growth unfold before your eyes. See instructions for forcing bulbs on next page.

All you need is …
potting soil; 3 to 5 cylinder vases, preferably the same height; bulbs in bloom; faux snow (optional)

All you do is …
place 2 in./5 cm of soil in each vase. Remove the flowers from their containers and trim extra roots, leaving about 1.5 in/4 cm. of roots. Place the bulbs on top of the soil and add more soil so the roots are covered. Water … and you are done!

Faux snow is a powder that turns into snow when you add water. Sprinkle it on the flowers. Some of the snow will fall on the soil, creating a wonderful effect.

Mix water with some faux snow for an indoor spring storm.

To force bulbs …

take bulbs that have been kept in cold storage over the winter and plant them in vases, covering with soil. Water lightly. Keep the vases in a cool place with some light for about two weeks to develop roots. Water when needed. Bring into sunlight, keep watering and revel in the joy of spring!

It takes just minutes to transfer plants into vases.

17

Start with your mother's favourite colour of roses.

roses for mum

My mum loved roses. Every free moment was spent in her rose garden, attending to them, weeding them or simply admiring them. I'm sure she even talked to them. When the weight of the world rested heavily on her shoulders, she would escape to her garden for the therapeutic medicine that only her roses could offer. The sight of roses never fails to remind me of my mother. She would have loved to have lunch with me at this table!

All you need is …
your mother's favourite colour of roses, buds and blooms; 2 inserts; 1 cylinder vase; 1 large floating candle

All you do is …
trim the roses so they fit snugly in the inserts.
Fill the vase with water and add the candle.
If you have any extra blossoms, scatter their petals around the centrepiece.

Rose-patterned plates reflect the theme.

cheery chicks

Have you ever watched a flock of chicks? They're constantly moving, chirping and jumping.

That's what ours are doing on the Easter brunch table. One has jumped on an egg cup that holds a boiled egg, one is perched on top of a stack of eggs and jelly beans, and two chicks are trying to kiss through the glass! And jelly beans everywhere—they've made such a pretty mess! It's a good thing the glass vases keep them contained … just barely.

All you need is …
1 egg cup; eggs; 4 chicks; 3 cylinder vases; jelly beans

All you do is …
place an egg cup, topped with an egg and a chick, in one vase and a single chick in another. Put five eggs with a chick on top in a third vase. Place the fourth chick facing the vase that has a single chick at the bottom. Keep your eye on those two! Add some jelly beans to the vases and sprinkle the rest on the table.

Stack an egg cup, egg and a chick in a vase and add coloured jelly beans.

20

Set an additional
chick on the
table to face its
friend in the
vase so they
can visit. What
a friendly flock!

branches in bloom

Attach a twig to the bird's beak with a glue gun and she is ready to build her nest.

Start spring early by forcing flowering branches to bloom. Then make them the centre of a whimsical arrangement that will banish winter woes.
Snip off branches from your favourite flowering tree—forsythia, red dogwood, crabapple or cherry, for example. Cut them long enough to give an eye-catching height to your grouping.

All you need is …
freshly cut branches; 3 cylinder vases of different heights; tulip; 1 floating candle; tray; stones or polished pebbles; small ceramic bird

All you do is …
place the branches, with some water, in your tallest vase. Put the tulip in the medium vase. Float the candle in the shortest one. Display the vases on a charger plate, tray or placemat surrounded by polished pebbles. Use a glue gun to attach a twig to the beak of the bird and then place it on the tray.

The branches, pebbles and raffia tray give this centrepiece a natural look.

23

Use branches to support the weight of the clothes pegs.

24

new addition

One memorable day my daughter invited me out for coffee. I was surprised when she handed me a small, beautifully wrapped gift. In it was a tiny angel holding a star with the words: Expect A Miracle. She was expecting a baby! So much joy! And so much laundry! What a fun theme for a shower to welcome the new addition.

All you need is . . .
pastel wrapping paper; hole punch; 2 cylinder vases; branches spray-painted white, 10 yd./9 m pastel-coloured ribbon; mini-clothes pegs; teacup; flowers; shoebox wrapped in pastel paper; children's tea set

All you do is . . .
use the patterns on page 104 to draw baby clothes on the wrapping paper. Cut them out and decorate with the hole punch (see photos). Cut two paper strips from the wrapping paper to fit around your vases. Allow 1.5 in./4 cm of glass to show at the top of the vase and 3/8 in./1 cm to show at the bottom. Decorate the edges with the hole punch. Tape the paper around the vases. Fill them with branches and place them on your table. Now comes the fun part: use the ribbon to create a laundry line between the two "trees." Allow the ribbon to dip and flow between the branches. Attach the clothing to the ribbon, using the branches to support the pegs and ribbon. Fill the teacup with flowers and place on the wrapped box. Add the tea set. Wrap a ribbon around a napkin and cake fork. Add a final touch by writing each guest's name on a clothespin and clipping it to a napkin. Can you feel the love for the new addition?

25

fragrant and friendly

Take a close look at a hyacinth. Have you ever wondered how a single bulb can produce dozens of mini-flowers attached to one stem? Each one is a perfect beauty, ready for us to enjoy with friends.

All you need is …
sticky wax; 3 purple tapered candles; 3 cylinder vases; 1 hyacinth plant in full bloom; chopsticks or long tweezers; place cards; hole punch; purple ribbon

26

One single hyacinth bloom provides enough flowerets for the entire tablescape.

All you do is …

attach sticky wax to the bottom of the candles and place one in the centre of each vase. Gently "dismantle" a hyacinth bloom by snipping off individual flowerets and placing them around each candle. Using chopsticks, coax some of the blossoms to face outwards. Finish by sprinkling blooms around the centrepiece.

To make the individual place-card holders, tuck a single blossom into a hyacinth leaf (a dab of glue may be helpful). To attach the leaf and bloom to the place card, make two holes about 0.25 in./0.5 cm apart with the hole punch in the bottom corner of the card. Now place the leaf between the two holes, pass a ribbon through the holes and tie it behind the card. This should hold the leaf snugly in place.

A ribbon threaded through two holes in a place card holds a hyacinth leaf and blossom in place. Set it in a beautiful place-card holder and you're done.

bright and beautiful

Warm up a cool spring night with candlelight and the warm bright colours of primula plants—one of the first signs of spring. Match their shades to the pillar candles and tie the whole arrangement together with raffia and some Easter ornaments.

All you need is …
raffia; 3 to 5 primula plants; tiny eggs; 3 cylinder vases; 3 pillar candles; bunny figurine

Twist raffia in a circular motion to create a birds' nest. Dab with your glue gun as needed.

All you do is …
tie two to three strands of raffia together and attach them to the top of the plant pots with a glue gun. Wrap with the raffia and glue as required. Make a nest by starting with a tiny centre and wrapping raffia in larger and larger circles, gluing as needed. Add the eggs. Wrap raffia around the vases and insert the candles. Add the bunny to the display, or make a large nest by circling the bunny, a vase and a primula pot with raffia.

Make a large nest by wrapping raffia loosely around several objects. No glue required!

29

bouquet of carrots

You can't help but smile when looking at these bunnies. This simple arrangement could adorn your coffee table when you invite friends for nibblies or you can use it as a tablescape for a casual dinner party.

All you need is ...
carrots with fresh tops; 1 tall cylinder vase; 2 inserts; carrot sticks; dip; bunnies

All you do is ...
place a bunch of carrots with fresh tops in your vase. Fill one of the inserts with carrot sticks and the other with dip. Place bunnies at the base of the vase and scatter carrot greens among them. Use the glue gun to attach one carrot, with top, to the large bunny.

Help a bunny sink her teeth into a carrot by taking a small nibble before placing it in front of her.

magic memories

Memories of forget-me-nots ... do you recall them growing in your grandmother's garden? Do you remember giving a bouquet to a special person or finding them tucked in a letter from an admirer? This tiny, beautiful, unpretentious flower has a wonderful power to help bring back magical memories! Create your own special memories with these delicate forget-me-nots and a few vases. Then pause and reflect on your own remembrances of things past, or invite a friend for tea and an unforgettable afternoon.

All you need is ...
forget-me-nots; 2 cylinder vases; 2 blue floating candles; 2 inserts

All you do is ...
place three to four forget-me-nots in the first vase. Fill with water, stopping 1.25 in./3 cm from the top of the vase. Place a floating candle on top. Fill an insert with forget-me-nots and add water. Fill the second vase with 1.25 in./3 cm water. Cut forget-me-nots to 3-in./7.5-cm lengths and add. Place an insert filled with water on top. Add a floating candle.

Someone once wrote that memories are like jewels that we collect throughout our lives. Dry forget-me-nots by placing them between paper and tucking them in a book.

33

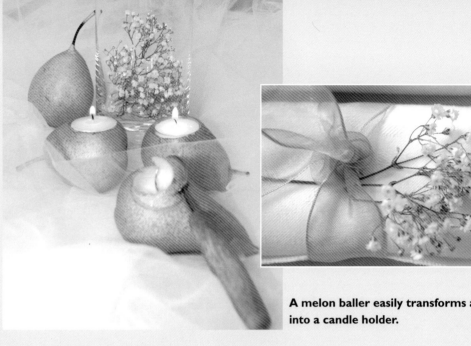

A sprig of baby's breath adds the finishing touch to a napkin.

A melon baller easily transforms a pear into a candle holder.

the perfect "pair"

This is a great idea for an engagement party or bridal shower. Congratulate the lucky pair with a playful display of fresh green pears that match the stems of the baby's breath and ribbon. There's nothing pared down about this centrepiece!

All you need is …
2 yd./2 m bridal tulle or white netting; 3 cylinder vases; green pears; 3 inserts; fresh baby's breath and other white flowers; green organza ribbon; melon baller; tea lights

All you do is …
cut three 8 x 8-in./20 x 20-cm pieces of tulle. Scrunch them up and place one in each vase. Place a pear in each vase on top of the tulle. Top with an insert and add fresh flowers. Scrunch up remaining tulle and place on the tablecloth to create a feeling of softness and freshness. Tie napkins with organza ribbon and tuck a spray of baby's breath in each. You may further the "paired" theme by tying two rings together with ribbon to display on the tulle (not shown). For innovative candle holders, use a melon baller to scoop out enough pear flesh to fit a tea light. Insert tea lights and prop the pears on your table, making sure they cannot roll around.

doves of love

Two white doves, symbolizing peace and love, rest on a cloud of stiff netting and set the scene for an anniversary or wedding. A contrasting tablecloth of royal blue makes your centrepiece stand out.

All the best to the loving couple!

All you need is . . .
3 pieces stiff mesh netting, 20 in./50 cm wide, of different lengths: 12 in./30 cm, 18 in./45 cm and 20 in./50 cm; 2 inserts; 2 cylinder vases, large and small; 1 ball candle; 2 doves; 1 white Asiatic lily

All you do is . . .
fold the finished edges of the 12-in./30-cm netting together, gather the edges and push them firmly into one insert. Allow some of the netting to puff over the top of the insert. Ensure unfinished edges are also tucked in. Roll the 18-in./45-cm piece tightly so it will fit into the small vase. Push two-thirds of the netting into the vase. Drape the remainder over the rim and hold it in place by pushing the other insert into the vase. Place the candle in the insert, ensuring the netting is safely out of reach of the candle.

Attach the doves with a glue gun. Place the lily in the second vase with some water. Place the vases and insert on the remaining netting, allowing it to roll or gather in a pleasing manner. A small dab from a glue gun can secure the netting to the vases.

gentlemen . . . start your engines

Totally casual and fun, this is perfect for Father's Day or Race Day. Yes, you can assemble this in minutes.

All you need is ...
black-and-white "racing" napkins or fabric; 1 cylinder vase; 1 short pillar candle; wheelbarrow tire; pie plate; toy cars and racing flags

This racy idea is sure to rev up any speed demon! A glass pie plate fits perfectly into the opening of a wheelbarrow tire.

All you do is …
randomly cut out black squares on paper napkins with scissors to allow some light through. Wrap napkins around the vase and tape in place. Insert the candle. Place the wheelbarrow tire on your table and fit the pie plate inside the tire. Fill with snacks and don't forget to fill those glasses! Scatter racing cars and flags around the table.

39

Summer

These napkin rings double as tiny vases. Fill with water, blue food colouring and a few sprigs of fresh flowers. Napkin-folding instructions are on page 105.

something blue

Weddings and engagements are extraordinary moments in our lives. A table set with care and attention will help to make the day memorable for the special couple and everyone involved. We've chosen blue for the ribbons and food colouring, but you can change this to suit your decorating scheme . . .

All you need for each table of six guests is …
4 yd./4 m blue organza ribbon, 1 in./2.5 cm wide; 3 cylinder vases preferably the same height; spray adhesive; 1 yd./1 m jewelled ribbon; blue food colouring; pitcher; 3 large floating candles; 3 roses; 1 hydrangea flower, separated; 3 inserts; 6 glass napkin rings; 6 pieces of blue organza ribbon, 14 in./35 cm long, 3/8 in./1 cm wide; 6 place cards

All you do is …
cut the 1-in./2.5-cm-wide organza ribbon to fit around the rim of each vase, allowing for a small overlap. Run the remaining ribbon down the centre of the table. Place the three pieces of organza ribbon on newspaper and spray with glue. Attach them to the top of the vases. Cut the jewelled ribbon to fit around each vase. Using a glue gun, attach the jewelled ribbon just below the organza ribbon.

Add two drops of food colouring to a large pitcher of water. Place 1.5 in./4 cm blue water in each vase. Top with candles. Arrange one rose and some hydrangea blossoms in each insert. Alternate vases and inserts along the centre of the table.

Fill the glass napkin rings with blue water (a perfume funnel is helpful). Insert hydrangea blossoms into napkin rings. Fold napkins (see page 105 for instructions) and tuck into the rings. Tie the 14-in./35-cm ribbons through the top of each ring, right beside the blossoms. Place napkins on each dinner plate and prop a place card in a napkin fold.

For party favours …
place truffles in votive holders. Wrap the holders with tulle squares and tie with satin ribbon. Add a jewel removed from your jewelled ribbon if you wish.

Use mini-flags as picks for your food.

All you need is …
2 floating candles; 2 cylinder vases; curling ribbon; tiny Canadian cocktail flags; red-and-white napkins; 8-in./20-cm Canadian flag on a stick; red paper plates; large Canadian flag; red-and-white balloons

All you do is …
place candles in the vases. Tie curling ribbon around vases and insert small flags between the glass and the ribbon. Place your food in containers that are decorated with a napkin and cocktail flag and tied with ribbon. Poke a larger flag into your picnic basket. Serve food on red paper plates. Push cocktail flags into potatoes, pickles, hot dogs or hamburgers. Use them as picks for finger food. Complete the Canada Day look by draping a flag over the basket and table and adding red-and-white balloons.

o … canada

We often take our beautiful country for granted. When our children were young we travelled to Poland frequently to spend time with my family. At the time, Poland was a communist country with long lineups for scarce goods. Upon returning from one of these visits, our son, then 4, stepped off the plane and proudly proclaimed, "My Canada!" I must say that I feel much the same when I return from my travels. O … Canada, my wonderful country; my home!

Let's make Canada Day special and celebrate it with an all red-and-white picnic. For this event, vases become hurricane lamps, protecting the candles inside from unexpected gusts of wind.

O … CANADA … LET'S CELEBRATE FOR THEE!

For a dramatic display, use vases to elevate tea-time treats, but be sure to do your pie slicing on a steady surface.

tea under the tree

Don't let these ladybugs get away! Capture them in cylinder vases and invite them to tea. It's easy to do and so much fun for children and adults alike. Ladybugs are everyone's favourite so they can be purchased readily in gift shops and supermarkets. If there are none to be found, you and your family can use craft paint and beach stones to create your own unique ladybugs.

A garden hat can serve as a unique tray for inserts filled with tea fixings.

A bit of sand or crushed shells on the bottom of each vase shows off the ladybug.

All you need is …

sand or crushed seashells, available in pet stores; 3 cylinder vases; ladybugs of various sizes; greenery (trim your favourite garden plants!); serving tray; tea and treats

All you do is …

put sand in vases. Place a ladybug on top of the sand … be gentle! Add a green spray to each vase and secure it by pushing the stem into the sand. Place one vase on a tray and arrange treats around it. Top the vases with a pie or a plate containing additional treats. Scatter greenery around the tray and add any ladybugs you may have left.

Have fun painting ladybugs on beach stones!

49

Make your lotions special by attaching some pretty shells to the lids.

bathing beauties

Seashells ... such little houses for such tiny creatures! So much fun to collect! Picture yourself walking along the beach, the warm sun on your face and the sand under your toes. You become so intent on digging out a shell that you're oblivious to the waves washing across your feet. And what a beautiful treasure you've found! To capture past holidays for future remembrances, display your seashells in your bathroom.

All you need is ...

4 cylinder vases; perfumed soaps; bath beads; bath salt; shells; small scoop; starfish; I insert, I tea light, votive candles; large shallow shells; sea sponges

All you do is ...

use your vases to hold your soaps, bath beads, bath salt and shells. Add the scoop to the bath salt. Scatter starfish at the base of the vases. Add the insert, with tea light, to a vase. For special occasions, light candles (preferably in the same colour as the bath beads and bath salt) and nestle them into some bath salt on shallow shells. Decorate with starfish and sea sponges.

Use a glue gun to attach some starfish or seashells to your wall, mirror frame or picture frame.

51

To continue the sunflower theme, place extra sunflower leaves between dinner plates and salad plates.

sunny blooms

The first time I saw a field of sunflowers, I was travelling through Spain. I will never forget the sight: tall blooms reaching for the sky, their cheerful faces turned towards the sun. It was an endless expanse of sunshine that touched the horizon. To bring the feeling of sunshine to your table …

All you need is …
6 sunflowers: 3 with small blooms, 3 with large blooms; 3 inserts; 3 cylinder vases; 5 glass bowls, 2-in./5-cm diameter; 5 yellow floating candles; 5 small sunflower leaves

All you do is …
trim the smaller sunflowers, leaving no stem on one, a 1.5-in./4-cm stem on the second, and a 2.5-in./6-cm stem on the third. Place the sunflower heads in your inserts. Trim the fourth sunflower so it fits inside one of your vases. Trim the fifth so that the flower head rests on the vase rim. The last flower head should reach out past the top of the vase. Add a small amount of water to each bloom.
Fill the glass bowls with water. Add the floating candles and small sunflower leaves. Arrange sunflowers and candles on the table. WOW!

fruits of summer

A medley of pleasurable experiences awaits guests at a table set for alfresco dining. The colourful surroundings, the scent of the flowers and the sound of birdsong at sunset are a feast for the senses. Does it get better than this?

All you need is ...
4 cylinder vases of the same height; blueberries; strawberries; oranges; tray (preferably glass); 1 pillar candle; ivy; 3 colourful flowers (artificial blossoms work well); 1 insert; 1 blueberry-coloured floating candle; more blueberries

All you do is ...
fill one vase with blueberries, another with strawberries and the third with oranges (or use other combinations of fruit). Place the glass tray over the vases. Slip the pillar candle inside the fourth vase and centre it on the tray. Wrap strands of ivy around the vase with the pillar candle. Tuck the flowers into the ivy. Fill an insert three-quarters full with blueberries and place a candle on top. Add blueberries to the top of the candle and set the insert on the tray.

I used blueberries in this insert, but the possibilities are endless. Use whatever is in season!

Shoes on the table? Perfect for a soccer party.

"Dress" your vases in socks.

what a kick!

Shoes and socks on the table? It's unusual but perfect for an end-of-season soccer party. Or change to cleats and cheer on a football team! You can be sure all of your guests will get a kick out of this display. As an option, create that on-field look by placing the vases on a piece of turf, available at any hardware store. Cut it with scissors to the size and shape of your choice.

All you need is ...
2 cylinder vases; sports socks; soccer shoes; curling ribbon; 2 floating candles; soccer ball; letters to spell the word "kick"; inserts

All you do is ...
"dress" your vases in socks. Replace the laces in the soccer shoes with ribbon. Put the vases inside the shoes. Fill the vases with water and add candles. Place next to a soccer ball and arrange the letters to spell "kick". Serve veggies and dip in the inserts.

57

all aboard!

My dear friends, Akke and Reid, "showed me the ropes" when I first arrived in Canada years ago. Avid sailors, they now spend their winters in the Caribbean. Wouldn't it be nice to join them? Let this nautical theme whisk you away to an ocean adventure. Gift shops, party stores and even toy stores will often carry the life preservers, sailboats and lighthouses you'll need.

All you need is …
red construction paper; 4 toothpicks; sailboats: 4 small and 1 large; 11 ft./3.35 m red rope, 3/8 in./1 cm thick; 2 cylinder vases; 2 small life preservers, large enough to fit around your vases; 2 lighthouse statues; 2 red floating candles

All you do is …
cut flags from the red paper using the pattern on page 104. Write your guests' names on the flags. Use the toothpicks to attach them to the top of each small sailboat as place cards. Cut two pieces, 26 in./66 cm long, from the rope and tie reef knots on the vases. You will need 20 in./50 cm of rope for each napkin ring. Tie a reef knot around each napkin.

Arrange the large sailboat, life preservers and lighthouses on your table. Fill the vases with water and a candle. Fit them into the life preservers. Place the small sailboats on top of the napkins.

To make a reef knot, pass the right end over the left and then under it. Then pass the left end over the right and under it. Tighten by pulling the ends. Or see drawings on page 104.

Fall

party with presence

I love to give lots of gifts; I love to receive lots of gifts … and I love this birthday decorating idea that features lots and lots of presents. Assemble this while you're watching your favourite show and you'll be done in no time.

All you need is …
Styrofoam or toy blocks; sheets of brightly coloured paper; curling ribbon; 3 cylinder vases; 3 inserts; 3 tea lights

All you do is …
with a sharp knife, cut Styrofoam into various rectangular and square pieces no larger than 2 x 1.5 x 0.75 in./5 x 4 x 2 cm. If you prefer, use children's blocks. Wrap them in colourful paper and tie with curling ribbon. Fill the vases with the gifts, leaving enough space for an insert. Top with an insert and place a tea light inside. Scatter extra tiny presents (and perhaps a few real ones!) at the base of the vases.

oceans of glass

When you find objects that you admire, consider using them for decorating. Since I loved the shapes and colour of large chunks of sea glass, my thoughts turned automatically to tablescaping with them. Wrapping soft aluminum wire around them makes them both decorative and useful. Now you can use them to support a candle, hold a flower, or make an unusual napkin ring! Suspend sea glass pieces in a window to catch a shining ray or hang them above your table to reflect the candlelight.

Glass pieces wrapped with wire can be suspended with fishing line.

All you need is …

soft aluminum wire; large chunks of coloured sea glass; sticky wax; 2 tapered candles (preferably to match the colour of the daisy); 3 cylinder vases of the same height; 1 artificial gerbera daisy

All you do is …

wrap wire around sea glass chunks to create patterns that please your eye. Place sticky wax on the end of the candles and place them in the centre of two vases. Insert the gerbera daisy into the third vase. Place the wire-wrapped sea glass around the candles and the gerbera daisy, ensuring that the candles stand upright. Place additional pieces of sea glass around the vases and consider hanging some outside the tops of the vases.

65

martini madness

Cool enough even for James Bond! This icy martini bar features two vases nestled in crushed glass, ice, and key limes.

All you need is …

coarse sea salt (or crushed glass); rectangular glass dish, just big enough to hold inserts; 3 inserts; martini condiments; 2 cylinder vases; 2 blue tea lights; 2 expandable bracelets; 4 cups/1 L crushed turquoise glass; shallow, clear bowl or high-rimmed tray; 6 mini-limes; ice

All you do is …

place 2 in./5 cm sea salt or crushed glass in rectangular dish. Add the inserts, filled with martini condiments. Anchor the condiments by pushing them slightly into the salt or crushed glass. Put 1.25 in./3 cm sea salt in the bottom of each vase and top with a tea light. Dress the tops of the vases with the bracelets, twisting and turning them till they please your eye. Place turquoise glass in the shallow bowl and add the vases and limes. Just before your guests arrive, add lots of ice and light your candles.

Set inserts in a bed of sea salt. Sidewalk salt works too!

The dramatic combination of fire and ice makes for a constantly changing display as the cubes crack, move and melt and the limes float through the ever-rising water. What a show!

67

Use extra painted poppy pods as place-card holders. Notch them with a knife and insert the cards.

Fiona

poppy power

Poppy pods are beautiful in their natural state but a dash of colour makes an eye-popping display. Craft and decorating stores carry painted poppy pods. Or spray paint them to achieve your favourite colour.

All you need is …
21 poppy pods; raffia or ribbon; 3 cylinder vases of equal height; 4 inserts; 4 autumn leaves (real or artificial); 4 red floating candles

All you do is …
cut all pods to a height of 14 in./35 cm. Tie seven pods with raffia 6 in./15 cm from the bottom. Separate the cut ends to create a teepee. Repeat with remaining pods. Place the pods in vases and centre them on your table.
Wrap raffia three times around each insert and push a leaf or sprig between the raffia and the insert. Put candles inside the inserts and add to your table.

Place neatly folded napkins on dinner plates. Top the napkins with real or artificial leaves and cover with glass salad plates.

69

spice up your life

Add some spice to cool fall days with spicy food, spicy decorations …
and spicy conversation. Remember to test your spices on a cloth before
scattering them on your tablecloth so that you don't stain an heirloom!

All you need is …
2 brown paper lunch bags; 3 cylinder vases of different heights; 2 large
orange floating candles; 1 cup/250 mL red chili peppers; votive holder;
votive candle; cinnamon sticks; 5 small brown paper bags, 3.5 x 6.5 in./9
x 16 cm; whole nutmeg; star anise; cardamom pods; bay leaves; oregano
twigs; 12 tiny brown paper bags, 2.5 x 3.75 in./6 x 10 cm; 4 inserts

All you do is …
create a cuff on the large bags by making a 1-in./2.5-cm fold and turning
it twice. Place one small and one large vase in these two bags. Add floating
candles. Push the tops of bags down to give them a crumpled look. Place
the chili peppers in the medium vase and push the votive holder with a
votive candle inside the vase. Place several cinnamon
sticks between the votive holder and vase.

Create a cuff on one small bag. Fill with spices
and lay it on its side so that spices appear to spill
out. Repeat with four tiny bags for your centrepiece.
Cut the top and bottom of four tiny bags to
produce 1.5-in./4-cm-wide napkin ring bands. Roll
your napkins tightly and slide them in. Scatter the
table with spices. Fill tiny bags with remaining spices
and place on plates for your guests to take home.
Serve your starter in an insert wrapped in a small
paper bag.

**Tuck cinnamon sticks and oregano twigs between the
bags and vases of your centrepiece.**

71

bountiful thanks

It's Thanksgiving—a time to gather with family and friends and to reflect on the blessings we have received. What a joyful bounty!

All you need is …
3 cylinder vases; 1 pumpkin, 12-in./30-cm diameter; large platter; 3 inserts;
3 votive candles; 1 butter squash; 2 to 5 assorted gourds; fall leaves and berries; 2 small pumpkins, 6-in./15-cm diameter; bead wax and wick

All you do is …
place one vase on top of the big pumpkin and trace the base with a felt pen. Scoop out the circle and place the tallest vase in the hole. Set the pumpkin on the platter, ensuring it is stable. Arrange the remaining vases, inserts with candles, squash, gourds, leaves and berries on the platter. Scoop out the top of the small pumpkins. Add bead wax and wick and set the pumpkins out as additional sources of light!

Pears make perfect place cards.

73

Pumpkins are such cheery, friendly vegetables. Choose ones with different stem lengths for added interest.

pumpkins aplenty

Pick some small pumpkins and arrange them on your table, mantel or windowsill early in the fall. Feast your eyes on your colourful display till Halloween.

All you need is ...
3 birch logs, 1.5 in./4 cm long; 2 birch logs, 2.75 in./7 cm long; 2 birch logs, 3.5 in./9 cm long; 6 miniature pumpkins; 3 cylinder vases; 3 pillar candles; 6 artificial fall leaves; adhesive spray

All you do is ...
experiment with your birch logs and pumpkins, arranging them to your liking. Place the vases with the pillar candles where you like, or follow the pattern on the picture provided. Place the leaves on newspaper, spray with adhesive and attach them to your vases. Enjoy the warm glow on a cool autumn evening!

75

under the tuscan sun

As part of my fundraising commitment to Edmonton's Stollery Children's Hospital Foundation, I design tablescapes to be raffled. This Tuscan-inspired display, with its cheery sunflowers and bright citrus fruit, seems to put a smile on everyone's face.

All you need is …
1 birch log, 6 in./15 cm high, 9-in./23-cm diameter, or a small wooden wine crate; 1 large circular platter; 3 cylinder vases; 3 large yellow floating candles; artificial grapevines; artificial olive twigs; 7 artificial sunflowers; 9 ceramic oranges (real ones work too!)

Write your guests' names on artificial sunflower leaves and tuck them into the grapevine at each setting.

All you do is …

place the log in the centre of the table and top with the platter. Add water to the vases and balance carefully on the platter. Add the candles to the vases. Wind the grapevine through the display, allowing it to flow off the platter and above the vases. Tuck the olive twigs into the display. Arrange sunflowers and three oranges on and around the platter.

Wrap the remaining oranges with grapevines and place on a napkin at each setting.

Let the grapevine extend above the vases for dramatic flair.

77

scary nights

Ghosts and goblins come out to play and have a wickedly good time! Set the scene for Halloween …

All you need is …
black tablecloth; 1 sturdy shoebox; 2 yd./2 m black tulle; pumpkins and gourds; artificial leaves; 3 cylinder vases of different heights; orange acrylic ice or glass gems; 3 small yellow floating candles; 1 scary votive holder; 1 ghost or other Halloween figurine; 1 insert; 1 yd./1 m orange fabric or handmade paper; lampshade kit; plastic creepy crawlies

All you do is …
cover your table with the black tablecloth. Slip the shoebox under the tablecloth. Scrunch up the tulle and place on top. Place the pumpkins and gourds randomly on the table. Tuck some leaves under the tulle and into folds; scatter the rest. Cover the bottom of the vases with acrylic ice. Fill the smallest vase with water and top with a candle. Add the votive holder, with candle, to the medium vase. Place figurine and insert, with candle, in tall vase.
Cut out an orange cover for the lampshade. (The pattern is enclosed when you buy a kit.) Place the shade on top of the tall vase. Add creepy crawlies to the shade with a glue gun. Place the vases on or beside the shoebox.

"Spook"-y accents are readily available before Halloween.

Winter

Float artificial pearls in vases of water tinted with blue food colouring and add a floating candle.

tempting treasure

The mystery of sunken riches, mermaids swimming in the ocean blue, seashells revealing tales of rowdy pirates … just the tropical centrepiece to lure party-goers on a cold winter's evening.

All you need is …
craft paper; felt pen; spray paint; play jewelry; blue food colouring; 3 cylinder vases; 3 blue floating candles; blue or aqua tablecloth; gold foil-wrapped chocolate coins; seashells; family treasures

All you do is …
to create the mermaids, follow the pattern on page 104, enlarging it so the circle fits snugly around the vase.

Gather all your treasures: old coins, tarnished cutlery and the family's silver teapot hiding in the closet!

Cut the mermaids out and decorate with a felt pen and spray paint. Place the play jewelry in the vases. Add water to the vases and tint with the blue food colouring. Slide your mermaids over the vases and add floating candles. Ensure that your mermaids do not get in the way of the candles. Place vases on the tablecloth and scatter more jewelry, gold coins and seashells at the base of the vases.

83

Create a wreath at the base of vases and inserts by wrapping them with ivy.

dinner at eight!

I ran into dear friends late one afternoon, and invited them for dinner that evening. My favourite deli would take care of the food, but what about a centrepiece? All I had was an exuberant ivy plant and some carnations. Hmmm …

All you need is …
7 carnations; ivy plant; 6 cylinder vases; 3 inserts; 9 large tea lights

All you do is …
cut the petals off the carnations. Give your ivy plant a haircut by trimming its longest strands. Make a layer of carnation petals 1.25 in./3 cm deep in the vases and inserts. Nestle the candles inside the petals. Line up the inserts at the centre of the table and group three vases at each end. Wrap ivy around each vase and insert. Place napkins in water glasses and wrap ivy around each napkin.
It's only 7 p.m. … plenty of time to pick up my deli order and powder my nose!

85

glowing embers

It's cold and snowy outside—a perfect day to curl up with a good book and warm blanket. Turn your vases into lanterns, settle down with some chocolate and a glass of liqueur and watch the evening descend from your cozy nook.

You can find beautiful decorative paper at art supply shops or craft stores. Look for it in the scrapbook or card-making section.

All you need is …
1 large pretty sheet of decorative paper, layered with cedar or fir needles; 3 cylinder vases of the same height; raffia; 3 votive candles

All you do is …
cut three pieces of paper as wide as each vase is high and just long enough to wrap around each vase. Wrap the paper around the vases and tape in place. Wrap raffia around the top and tie it securely. Add the candles.

If you catch yourself lost in a book till dinnertime, bring your lanterns to your dining table to serve as a centrepiece. Scatter chunks of bark to add interest. Write your guests' names on flat pieces of bark using a gold calligraphy pen.

cool cranberries

I am not sure what I like best about cranberries—their deep, rich colour; their tart, lively taste; or the fact that they last so long on the branches in this project. Stock up so you can freshen up the cranberries in the vases and inserts.

FOR THE TABLE DISPLAY
All you need is …
3 cylinder vases; 1 package of fresh cranberries; spray-on snow; 3 inserts; 3 red floating candles; small branches; nail; 12 artificial mini-apples

All you do is …
fill vases one-third full of cranberries. Spray snow on one side of the vases, tapering it down so that it appears like a snow drift. Spray the rims of the inserts with snow and place them in the vases. Add water, candles and more cranberries to the inserts.
Spray snow on the branches and set them aside to dry. Use the nail to pierce more cranberries. Thread them onto the tips of your branches. Place them beside the vases. Spray the apples with snow and scatter among the branches.

FOR THE BUFFET DISPLAY
All you need is …
spray-on snow; small branches; 1 cylinder vase; 1/2 package of fresh cranberries; nail; cotton batting; 3 white ball candles; 3 inserts

All you do is …
spray snow on the branches and place them in the vase when dry. Pierce cranberries with the nail and slip them on the branch tips. Cut a piece of batting to suit and stretch it until it looks like snow. Lay it on the buffet. Add the candles to the inserts and place them on the batting. Add the vase. Sprinkle remaining cranberries around the inserts.

Now … doesn't this look cool?

To make a lemon pomander, score the lemon with a sharp knife to create rings around it. Press cloves into the rings. Tie a ribbon around the lemon.

scents of christmas

The scent of cinnamon brooms and fresh winter greenery permeates the house. Add a top note of holiday baking–some lemon-glazed stars or orange marmalade squares, perhaps? What a wonderful Christmas aroma!

All you need is …
2 rubber bands; 2 cylinder vases, large and small; 1 bundle of cinnamon sticks; red raffia; cedar boughs; tray or placemat; 1 Santa or other holiday figurine; 1 green apple; 1 orange; 1 lemon pomander; 1 red pillar candle

All you do is …
place one rubber band 1.5 in./4 cm from the bottom of the small vase. Place the second band 1.5 in./4 cm above the first one. Break some cinnamon sticks to create different lengths and wedge them under both rubber bands as pictured. Wrap a long strand of raffia tightly around the cinnamon sticks between the rubber bands. Tie the raffia ends together securely. Cut the rubber bands off.
Place cedar boughs on the tray or placemat. Add the Santa, vase and fruit. Put the pillar candle inside the vase. Create a background for your display by placing the large vase filled with Christmas greenery behind the small vase.

Use the rubber bands to hold the cinnamon sticks in place before wrapping them in raffia.

90

berry beautiful

Few things are more appealing than the scent and look of a wreath made with fresh greenery. With the help of an artificial wreath, this aromatic centrepiece is easily made.

All you need is …
1 artificial berry wreath; fresh greenery; 2 cylinder vases; 3 inserts; kumquats; 2 floating candles; small limes; apples

All you do is …
place your wreath on a tray. Cut the greenery and push it into the wreath, distributing it evenly. Add more greenery to the vases and top with inserts. Fill the inserts with several kumquats, a candle and water. Place the vases inside the wreath. Add more fruit and greenery around the vases. Finally, add the third insert filled with fruit, tipping it slightly. And now it's time to sit down and enjoy a glass of mulled wine or cranberry cider beside your berry beautiful creation.

93

a winter's tale

Snow is falling and the temperature is dropping … a perfect time for a cozy winter's tale–perhaps a story about three hardy souls who've ventured into the forest looking for a Christmas tree. Darkness falls … will the trio survive? Gather 'round the campfire for the rest of the fairy tale!

All you need is …
branches; waterproof tray; faux snow; 1 spruce branch; 1 cylinder vase; 2 inserts; 2 tea lights; 3 small figurines; tiny twigs; 1 battery-operated tea light; red curling ribbon; 16-in./40-cm length of soft wire

All you do is …
place the cedar branches on the tray and set it by a window. Add water to the faux snow according to package directions and pile it on the branches. Place some snow and the spruce branch inside the vase. Top with an insert and a tea light. Place the vase on the tray.
Set the figurines in a semi-circle on the tray. Build your "fire" by attaching the twigs to the battery-operated tea light with a glue gun. Set it in front of the figurines. Attach twigs to two of the figurines with the glue gun. Wrap a bundle of twigs with a small piece of ribbon and tie a bow.

Light the night by turning the second insert into a hanging lantern. Wrap it with wire, making two loops on opposite sides. Tie ribbon to the loops and suspend your lantern from the top of the window, next to the campsite. Add a little snow to the insert and place the second tea light on top. The glow from the "lantern" looks just as pretty from outside your home!

A battery–operated tea light makes a fabulous miniature fire. Glue twigs at an angle to make the "fire" look realistic.

95

These mice have teamwork down to an art.

'twas the night before christmas …

It's Christmas Eve and everyone is tired from cooking, baking, shopping and wrapping. They are all fast asleep. But wait! A few mice have stirred from their beds to do the last bit of decorating …

All you need is …
Artificial or real greenery; pine cones; berry branches; 1 cylinder vase; 2 bendable figurines, e.g.: mice, snowmen, angels; 1 candle, pear-shaped or votive; 1 insert; walnuts; place cards

All you do is …
place your greenery lengthwise in the centre of the table. Add cones and some berry branches for interest. Fill your vase with berry branches. Pose a figurine by the vase as if it were arranging some berries. Place the candle in the insert. Pose the second figurine as if it were holding the insert. Pry apart the walnuts slightly with a paring knife and push a place card into the opening. Put the walnut in a napkin folded into a triangle roll. (See page 105 for instructions.) Now it's time to sneak back into bed to dream of sugar plums and a happy Christmas!

96

**This is an evening of celebration.
The more stars the better!**

star of wonder

When I was a child we waited with bated breath for Christmas Eve's first star. Would it be Sirius or Betelgeuse? That first twinkle was the sign that our joyful celebrations could commence.

All you need is …
soft gold wire; 3 cylinder vases; gold stars; place cards; cedar boughs; 3 large gold tea lights; 3 inserts

All you do is …
create your own heavenly landscape by coiling the wire and twisting it inside, around, and outside the vases. Mark your orbits by gluing stars on the wire with a glue gun. Attach stars to place cards. Create a napkin ring by attaching two stars to a wire wrapped around a napkin. Spread the cedar boughs attractively on the table. Place the tea lights in the inserts, add them to the vases and prepare for a starry, starry night!

98

The moon, like a flower
In heaven's high bower,
With silent delight
Sits and smiles on the night.

They are designed to keep drinks cold, but battery-powered ice cubes also make wonderful decorations.

shooting star

When you wish upon a star … on New Year's Eve … and really believe … .
Well, let's set the scene for wishing first.

All you need is …
faux snow; 7 cylinder vases in assorted sizes; Christmas balls in 3 sizes from 1 in./2.5 cm to 3 in./7.5 cm; 42 pieces iridescent cello wrap, 3 × 5 in./7.5 × 13 cm; 7 pieces iridescent cello wrap, 8 × 8 in./20 × 20 cm; 7 battery-powered, flashing ice cubes or floating candles; 12 shooting stars: 6 stars, 5 in./13 cm long; 6 stars, 8 in./20 cm long

All you do is …
add water to the faux snow according to package instructions. Line up all your vases, decorations and snow for easy assembly. Place a large or medium-sized ball in each vase. Add a small piece of cello. Continue filling vases with smaller balls and small cello pieces until the vases are three-quarters full. Push a large cello piece into each vase to form a cup. Add snow to the cups. Top with ice cubes. Push stars randomly into the snow and scatter some balls on the table.

101

inspire with desire

The pop of a champagne cork, the glow of a candle, the tickle of a feather … all combine to inspire desire. Black lace, red boa … hearts are on fire!

All you need is …

1 ft./30 cm black lace, 3 in./7.5 cm wide; 1 cylinder vase; red boa; 20 x 20 in./ 50 x 50 cm clear cello wrap; large red floating candle; champagne bucket with ice; beluga caviar (just kidding!); person to inspire with desire!

All you do is …

wrap the lace tightly around the top of the vase. Hold it together with a straight pin, or glue it to the vase with a glue gun. Cut the red boa to fit around the base of the vase and secure with a straight pin. Push the cello wrap into the vase and fill with water. Top with the candle and place next to the champagne bucket. Don't save this just for Valentine's Day!

When you add water to the cello wrap, you'll create an icy fantasy.

Patterns

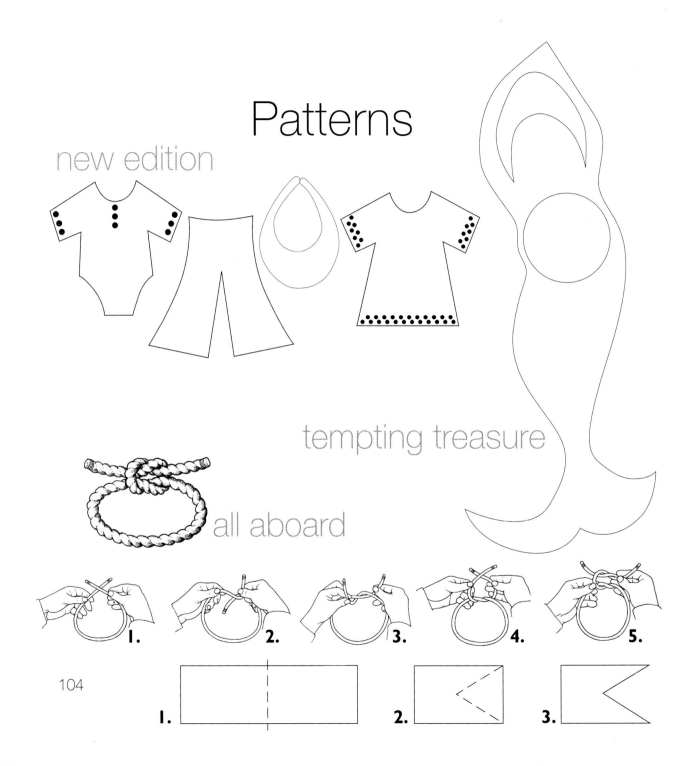

new edition

tempting treasure

all aboard

1.　　2.　　3.　　4.　　5.

104

1.　　2.　　3.

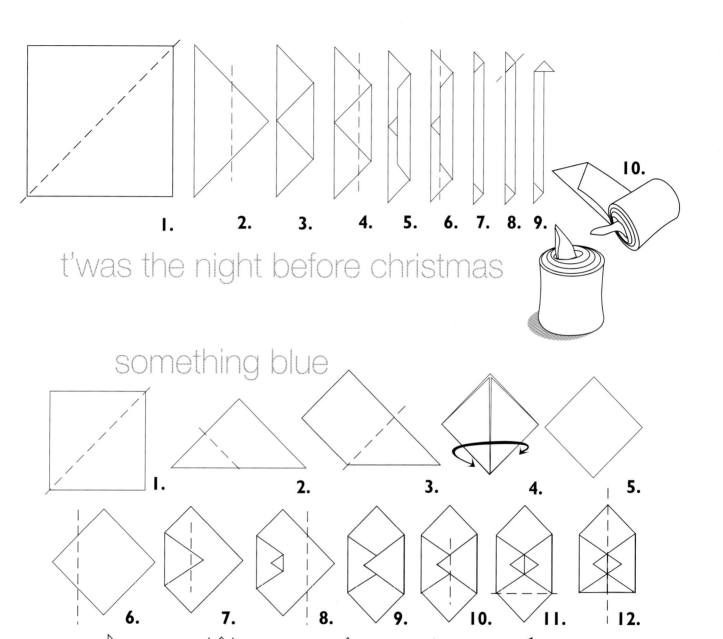

t'was the night before christmas

1. **2.** **3.** **4.** **5.** **6.** **7.** **8.** **9.** **10.**

something blue

1. **2.** **3.** **4.** **5.** **6.** **7.** **8.** **9.** **10.** **11.** **12.** **13.** **14.** **15.**

105